Understanding Organisation Culture

OrangeBooks Publication

1st Floor, Rajhans Arcade, Mall Road, Kohka, Bhilai, Chhattisgarh 490020

Website: **www.orangebooks.in**

© Copyright, 2024, Author

All rights reserved. No part of this book may be reproduced, stored in a retrieval system, or transmitted, in any form by any means, electronic, mechanical, magnetic, optical, chemical, manual, photocopying, recording or otherwise, without the prior written consent of its writer.

First Edition, 2024

ISBN: 978-93-6554-745-0

UNDERSTANDING ORGANISATION CULTURE

YOUR GUIDE TO CORPORATE SUCCESS

MANU KAUSHAL

OrangeBooks Publication
www.orangebooks.in

Organisation Culture

If you observe people who succeed in corporate life, you will note that they have an excellent understanding of the eco system. Gaining this knowledge takes years of effort. This book opens for you, the secret doors to the corporate ways of working.

I have been studying for over 2 decades the cultural traits of organisations, and their impact on the workforce. This study has helped many individuals through medium of corporate trainings and 1-1 coaching sessions. Time is apt now, to reveal it to a wider audience so that many more can benefit from this knowledge.

The approach behind this book is the fundamental scientific process that has been followed through ages.

Experimentation -> Observation -> Inference -> Prediction -> Validation.

There are many stories shared in this book that are based on real life experiences. Slight changes, if any, have been made to portray scenarios that would work best for readers. Any resemblance to any person is coincidental here.

Full of Vedic wisdom, real life stories, and easy to follow tips, this book will be your companion in the pursuit of corporate success and happiness.

Manu Kaushal
New Delhi, India
Email - manu5577.k@gmail.com

Content

Foreword viii

Prologue & Acknowledgements xi

Chapter 1 What Is Organisation Culture? 1

Chapter 2 Types of Organisations 10

Chapter 3 Know Yourself 19

Chapter 4 Observe & Understand 30

Chapter 5 What Will Not Work? 40

Chapter 6 What Will Work? 48

Chapter 7 Time Management 71

Chapter 8 Some Questions 78

Chapter 9 Notes for Senior Leadership 92

Chapter 10 Your Career Document 102

What Next To Expect From The Author 112

Foreword

By Professor S. Sadagopan

(I owe my IT career and corporate etiquette to him)

Prof Sadagopan was Director of IIITB from 1999 to 2021. He has taught at some of the most prestigious institutions, both in India and abroad (including IITs) and mentored some of the finest corporate brains.

It has been a delight to read **Understanding Organisation Culture** by Manu Kaushal. In an era where books on organisational culture abound, Manu brings a fresh, authentic perspective, grounded in over 25 years of closely observing the dynamics within organisations. What makes this book stand out is its genuine approach, infused with real-world insights and personal reflections that give readers a deep understanding of organisational nuances.

The inclusion of multiple quotes in Sanskrit adds a timeless touch, enriching the narrative and giving the reader a pause for reflection. These quotes, paired with insightful short stories, make the book both engaging and highly relatable, a rarity in a genre that often leans toward abstract theories.

Manu's genuine passion for the subject shines through every chapter. His ability to distil complex ideas into simple, actionable advice makes this book a must-read for students, professionals, and leaders alike. Whether you are new to the corporate world or a seasoned executive, this book provides valuable insights into why some thrive in certain environments while others struggle, despite equal talent and effort.

It is a treasure trove of wisdom for anyone eager to understand corporate politics, the impact of organisational culture on individual success, and how to navigate it all with integrity. I'm eagerly awaiting the print version, as there's something truly special about holding a book that offers both knowledge and inspiration.

Manu, your book is not just informative but truly heartfelt. It will undoubtedly resonate with many and become a go-to guide for those aspiring for corporate success.

Wishing you all the best,

Sadagopan

Prologue & Acknowledgements

वादे वादे जायते तत्वबोधः ।

*"It is only through the articulation of diverse opinion
that the truth will finally come out"*

This book is an honest attempt to speak what is not to be spoken. On organization culture, we either see books that establish ideals in theories, or those that are built on pure fiction. There are very few that are written with the purpose of learning, those that go beyond fiction or theory and talk about what actually happens in corporate world. For creating this book, I considered different real-life events and stories, brought in opinions and views of those involved, and then applied the test of logic to come up with explanations around organizational behaviours and patterns.

The inspiration comes from books like "Straight from the gut" and "What they don't teach at Harvard" that have dared to touch the sensitive subject of 'Ways of the Corporate World. The approach is practical, to the point (no circumventing), and with real life stories.

Even as individuals work hard to make their way up in corporate world, one often feels that individual growth and recognition is not proportional to talent, skill or even performance. Also, what works for one individual does not seem to work for another. And what works for one individual in one organisation does not seem to work for the same person in yet another organisation. What to do?

How to make sense out of this extremely confusing state of our industry?

Through this piece of work, I will explain the science behind what you see in the corporate world. It should help individuals understand why things happen the way they do. We will discuss things that confound, intimidate, and at times frustrate. And then the way out.

This book would not have been possible unless I had found Art of Living and followed teachings of His Holiness Sri Sri Ravi Shankar. Following him has given the physical, mental and spiritual strength to live life beyond the realm of comforts, wealth and pleasures.

I am very thankful to my sister, Shikha Punj, who has been my teacher since early school days, and who continues to guide me. She has helped me in reviewing and editing this book.

I also owe this book to my father, late Shri Sat Vrat Kaushal for motivating me to share the knowledge gained in the corporate world. During the early days of my career, I used to wonder how things happen in corporate world, and would often share with him. I had so many emotions, from despair to surprise, to disbelief to confusion. He would encourage me to record those incidents on paper. I still remember him say "My dear son, write down all that you are going through. Someday this will make a great read and help those who struggle to find their way through the corporate world. It will be your contribution and attempt to cleanse the corporate politics and bureaucracy."

For now, this is no attempt to clean the system. It is to first understand like a science student, how things work. And then to predict, and to find a clean way to survive, and succeed in your career.

Experimentation -> Observation -> Inference. I have used the same childhood science practical learnings to devise these techniques. I would encourage you to do the same. Read this book, experiment yourself, observe, infer, predict and act based on this knowledge. I am sure this will help you.

There are time tested tips and solutions that are included in each chapter of this book to ensure success for individuals as well as organisation leadership. Plus, it has real life stories to keep you amused.

Happy Learning!!

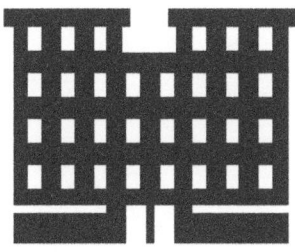

Chapter 1
What Is Organisation Culture? Can It Be Changed?

कः कालः कानि मित्राणि को देशः कौ व्ययागमौ ।
कश्चाहं का च मे शक्तिरिति चिन्त्यं मुहुर्मुहुः ॥

"Consider again and again the following: the right time, the right friends, the right place, the right means of income, the right ways of spending, and from whom you derive your power."

There is lot of material available on internet to describe culture, and more precisely Organisation culture.

I see it this way -

Organisation culture is the way things are done and understood in an organisation.

It includes the following:

1. The way of doing things.

2. The way people conduct themselves.

3. The way communication is carried out.

4. Vocabulary, or slangs used.

5. The core values that an organisation exhibits.

6. What is acceptable and what is not?

7. What is appreciated, what is rewarded, what is ignored, and what is punished?

8. What works and what does not work?

Organisations might not exhibit same behaviour and traits through its employees at hierarchy levels. The reason for this is that members at different levels have different set of priorities. The expectations from them are different since their maturity level and competence w.r.t. industry at large, might also vary. And most importantly, the version of truth might also be different, courtesy their access to certain facts.

As an example, a very simple etiquette like responding to a meeting invite, might never be honoured by a particular level of hierarchy while it might be binding on yet another level.

It is very important to understand that you would typically see some personal traits overriding the organisation culture. However, in most cases it is only a matter of time before individuals get overwhelmed by the culture.

Also, you will see members or groups strongly aligned, loosely aligned or in the middle of spectrum.

There could be some very strong personalities who would still resist the negative traits of the culture. Nevertheless, there would be some degree of impact on them as well.

It is also a fact that with organisation growth, and with new talent coming in, organisation culture undergoes transition. It also changes as the market demand changes.

However, that change has to be natural, and should evolve. It should not be in complete contradiction to the original organisation culture. Else, it would lead to disruptions. This artificial change is often seen during mergers and acquisitions, especially when there is a complete contrast between the value systems.

Let me give an example.

There was this widely admired big giant company that needed to expand its business to become bigger. It decided to merge with a less popular, yet a very successful firm that brought to it entry into an adjoining space, and helped it in expanding its business. However, the value systems across the two organisations were completely at odds. The smaller firm took pride in each individual that it had, and considered every individual in the organisation as a rare jewel. There was a lot of effort taken to hire each person, and they would never think of letting anyone go.

On the contrary, this giant company took pride in regular churn. They had this policy to identify the bottom few percent, moving them out of organisation and hiring another set to replace them. From a distance, this might sound abhorrent, considering there might be cases where this bottom might be doing things quite well and the replacement might end up with the company having individuals, who are not as skilled or talented. But this risk-taking ability was the hallmark of this giant firm. This is what a culture is all about. Over the years, members had come to live with this culture. Well, I am not talking about what is good or bad, it is more about what happens when contradictory cultures meet.

Now think of it, what would happen if one fine day this firm gets introduced to this culture of the giant.

The CEO of this firm was given the honour of heading the merged entity, but he ended up resigning. I remember his expressions when he shared his frustration with this entirely different culture. After that, it was only a matter of days before we heard of his resignation.

यथा राजा तथा प्रजा

"As the king, so are the subjects"

An important point to note regarding cultural change is that it has to always come from top. Top leadership has to really believe in it, and live by it. If leaders just wish the culture to change without bringing a change in themselves, it will not bring results.

Even if this condition that the leader has to believe in culture change, and follow it, gets satisfied, there is no guarantee that cultural change will indeed happen. Because it still depends on factors like how strong is the top, to what level he can go to implement the change, how rigid is the employee base, and how difficult it is to implement the change in view of the markets and business. But all said and done, the most influential person to implement a cultural change is that one person at the top. Not only should you know that change comes from top, you should also know that challenging this top into bringing a change on to themselves, can get you in deep trouble.

Let us go through a story to learn from history.

The story is about the great Greek Philosopher, Plato. Here is a king who is living a flamboyant lifestyle and calls Plato to his palace to implement his concept of Utopia, on to his kingdom. He gives Plato all the authority except that king himself should not be touched. To this, Plato responds by telling the king that the king himself has no belief or respect for Utopia, and is simply using it to go down in history, as someone who had got a great concept implemented.

With the king having an entirely different value system, the experiment was bound to fail. The only thing Plato didn't realize was that this kingdom did not even have a culture of openness. And Plato suffered due to this ignorance, or I would rather say due to his inability to comprehend the environment where he was. The king got him enslaved for his honesty.

In case you are curious to know what happened to Plato, note that he was finally freed by his pupils.

This entire breed of philosophers teaches us many important lessons. It shakes our value system (read Socrates dialogue with Creto around democracy). It also questions our capacity to take risk (read Spinoza). From Socrates to Plato to Aristotle, from teacher to student, each one of them was so much related to the other and yet so different, everyone was so brilliant.

You will be amused to know that there are so many learnings from the lives of great philosophers which are so very relevant in today's world. The extreme conditions of those different times, and respective philosophers' absolute love around their belief system, teaches us a lot. It also brings to our attention the importance of avoiding extremes.

I strongly recommend you go through 'Story of Philosophy' by Will Durant to get introduced to this subject.

But for now, let us go back to this very story and understand the lessons that we should learn in the context of corporate dynamics.

Here are the two important lessons:

One, Culture cannot be changed unless the top embraces it first.

Two, Honesty might be the best policy but how, when and in what way to tell the truth has to be based on organisation culture.

Plato got enslaved and **you could be fired** if you do not understand and practice this learning.

Chapter 2
Types of Organisations

गुणाः सर्वत्र पूज्यंते

"Virtue is adored everywhere"

Very often you see individuals switching companies for better salaries, designations, quality of work and work culture.

While the first two are very straight forward, the third one is a mirage and fourth one is best experienced.

We use a term 'cultural shock' to describe an immediate reaction that you experience for the first time, an entirely different culture, compared to what you have experienced in the past. But in reality, you rarely experience cultural shock. It seeps into your mind and heart over a period of time. And a moment comes when you start exhibiting the very same culture that you found strange in the beginning.

Good or bad, the fact is that it not only impacts your professional life but also your personal life. You are one person at the end of day, and any effort to split you into two, will be futile.

When you take a call on what organisation to join or leave, remember that this decision is going to impact you as a whole - the professional you, and the personal you.

Let us look at 12 characteristics of organisation by means of culture that they exhibit.

More often than not, you will see more than one such characteristic exhibited by a single organisation. It is very important that you understand the characteristics/ type of organisation before you join or before you decide to spend a lifetime with it. Otherwise, you will keep wondering, why it is not working out.

1. Organisations with strong risk appetite.

These are the ones where you can see young getting into challenging roles. These are also the ones that grow very fast and sometimes come down equally fast. They would churn out some strong industry leaders, and might redefine the way we work. Organisations that hire and fire, or the ones that segregate some low performance individuals and regularly churn them out belong to this category.

2. Organisations that are risk averse.

These are the ones that have a slow and steady story. They do grow, but then if you look closely, you would find that the growth should have been much greater. They will take years to crack a new client.

In these organisations, suggestions would be implemented based on who has given it, as they want to put effort only if it comes from people with tons of experience. This is because any change to them means unnecessary effort and risk. Here, the leadership does not believe that the new generation can be smarter than them. Suggestions are counted based on who gives them, and respect is given based on what salary is earned by the one suggesting the change.

3. Organisations that are people centric.

Happy faces, some really cool talent, less aggression, those who move slowly to pick up new and challenging opportunities. Work is regular and secure, but beware as changing markets might mean that they can be out of business.

Please be wary of organisations which say that it is people centric as well as client centric. Either it wants to be called people centric, while it is in reality client centric, or it wants to be called client centric while it is actually people centric, or it is in a state of confusion.

4. Organisations that are customer centric.

A shout from the customer in such cases would mean heads roll there, and personal commitments are kept aside.

Suggestion -> If you are in such an organisation, even if peers, team, and bosses provoke you, never become a reason for upsetting the client.

Chances are that same boss will dump you, when a client complaint comes against you.

When there is a customer situation, all hell would break loose, and with not so easy customers, such organisations end up producing angry managers and frustrated employees.

5. Organisations that strive on competence/ R&D.

Attractive place for talented people. Unless they are in market for a long time, or they are a small arm of a bigger umbrella company, they end up with short stunts. Great places to build CVs and to learn, but unless mapped to a more stable and practical mother organisation, they will not have a long play.

6. Organisations that are resource providers.

The ultimate purpose of business is to earn money with least pain. And that is what most service providers want. Albeit all the marketing campaigns and brand building activities done by such an organisation, you will not have to spend a lot of time to identify this type.

Let us do a quick test - Does this organisation always talk in terms of headcount? How much time is spent in meetings around hiring, attrition and resourcing? Here you go.

7. Organisations that live by short term goals.

These are typically started to make a quick headline, ensure good metrics for strong evaluation, and finally to get a good price. They would demand a lot of hard work from individuals with a promise of a bright future, but hidden behind is the real purpose and that is to sell off.

Well, if they get sold to bigger organisations that are really interested to cultivate the talent further, you might end up making it big. Otherwise, you might keep proving yourself over and over again, making you extremely frustrated and energy deprived. Here, your strategy should also be to play short.

8. Organisations that are long term players.

They have made a place for themselves in industry and would continue to enjoy this position for a long time. They are not confused around the business model, and as long as you align with them, you will have stability and long- term growth.

Such organisations generally do not offer either adventure or sharp learning curve. However, exceptions exist.

9. Organisations that are sales driven.

These are the ones where sales team leads and delivery team obeys. Most organisations are anyways driven by sales, but then sales team has limited understanding of the product and there should be someone at the top, who should be sane enough to understand this simple fact. He should be able to rein in Sales and Marketing to not oversell, and to sell right.

Your best bet in such a place is to be cozy with sales, and with the client. And then you are the king. Remember, sales team respects the one who is respected by client. Rest is all talk.

10. Organisations that are relationship based.

There are people who have mastered the art of creating relationships. Relationships alone cannot grow any company beyond a point. The inherent quality here is the strong C level connect. These companies will have limited growth. Sooner or later, they will need to inculcate some other organisation characteristics to grow further.

Hint - Company is there for a long time but growth is not as much. Brand name is not as popular. Here, sales heads have delivery backgrounds.

11. Organisations that are driven out of passion for the underlying product/ service.

Most startups are born out of passion for a product or business line. They bring on table lot of learning. If you are aligned to the vision, you will have excellent satisfaction levels.

But businesses run by passion mostly end up in dustbin. So, go short on it unless passionate executives are balanced by people with business sense.

If you have caught love bug, no advice can keep you away from your lover. So, enjoy it till the love lasts.

12. Organisations that are purely driven out of urge for bigger revenue and profits.

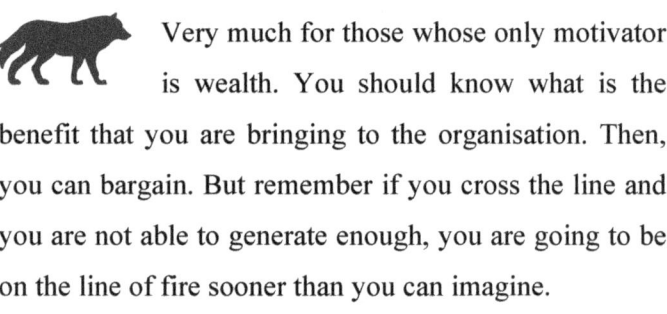

Very much for those whose only motivator is wealth. You should know what is the benefit that you are bringing to the organisation. Then, you can bargain. But remember if you cross the line and you are not able to generate enough, you are going to be on the line of fire sooner than you can imagine.

Chapter 3
Know Yourself

सर्वं परवशं दुःखं सर्वमात्मवशं सुखम् ।
एतद् विद्यात् समासेन लक्षणं सुखदुःखयोः ॥

"Everything that is in other's control is painful. All that is in self-control is happiness. This is the definition of happiness and pain in short."

In last chapter, we discussed different characteristics that are exhibited by organisations. By virtue of that, you can identify what type of organisation is yours, or what type of organisation you are getting into.

Let me be very categorical in saying that type of organisation has nothing to do with the presence or absence of politics. Some level of corporate politics will always be there. The question that you should answer is how much politics is there in your organisation? Is it evident everywhere? Is it in small pockets, and comes out on surface only a few times. Does it only appear if you put special effort to find out?

Are you someone who understands politics? Are you capable of playing it? Do you actually enjoy it? Based on what category you belong to, you can decide whether you should join a particular organisation, or if you should leave your current organisation.

To understand corporate politics, you need to stay tuned for my next book **"On Corporate Politics".**

For now, understand what skill comes naturally to you. If you are not good at corporate politics, my strong advice would be to stay away. Even if you try to play it, you will fail as someone with natural instincts is much smarter to understand, and thwart it. And then, he may use your misadventure to hit you really hard.

If you want to really play, be ready for bad reputation and multiple failures before you can drive it well.

My strong advice to "crying babies" is to stop cribbing about those who grow up the corporate ladder even with bad technical or people skills, and with bad performance. These are the people who spent as much time in studying and playing those chess moves while you were working for that project through late nights. And they might have been born with that skill that they nurtured in their past lives. While no textbook will tell you this, but it is a fact that corporate politics exists and is in plenty. You should at least understand it to an extent that it does not shock you. But let us turn back to the chapter theme.

Have you ever taken a course to understand your personality type? There are ample personality courses and books available that help you identify your type. Catch hold of one of them and spend a weekend on the subject. It is worth it! For beginners, let me give you a glimpse of it. Do revisit this section once you have gone through such a course or book.

Are you an analyst, or a charmer, a practical person or a dreamer?

You need to find out what you are good at. Are you smart, hard working or have talent to plan out a job like a game of chess?

What motivates you? Is it job security or adventure? Do you love number games or value play?

What is your communication style? Are you detail oriented? Or details threaten you?

Are you a charmer? Can you give this wonderful speech about a project team after doing quick 10- minute review with your project lead?

I would suggest that you should retrospect, and then introspect what type of person you are.

Look back and see at what point of time you were happiest.

What was the time when you were most miserable?

When did you achieve the most?

When were you most popular?

When were you appreciated?

You can possibly draw a time graph, and then answer each of the above questions for each year, or each span of few years.

Now, identify which part of your personality was at play. What was the kind of environment support you were getting during that period?

This will give you lot of insights about your inner self and validate the type of organisation environment that suits you.

But do not stop at the above retrospection. Now, go ahead and ask your peers, juniors and seniors to tell you what they think are your best strengths, and where they think you lag behind. Also, add a few family members and friends to this exercise. Because at the end of the day, you are one personality.

After you have collected all this feedback, ensure that you apply proper lens to throw away feedback that is given with set agendas.

 I remember a politically inclined person confiding in me during my initial industry days, when I was trying to settle in my career. He told me that feedback should be given depending on what we want to achieve out of it. He said that, this is what he has done throughout his career.

So, this particular person was a very accomplished lead. He tried to harm me for his rivalry with some senior manager who was seemingly close to me. But he could not destroy me, thanks to my hard work, skills and fame that I had already earned. And when I was no longer working with him, I went back to him to understand, why people do things which look so abhorrent at the first place. He looked to be a fairly good person, just that apart from other technical and soft skills, he considered politics as a very important tool needed to grow in profession.

You might think that this is a dirty conversation, but then the fact is that there are people who do it this way. We are not here debating whether people should give honest feedback or not. We are talking about a possibility that there are politically oriented people who will see this chance to give feedback as an opportunity to make a move.

And then there are members who would give feedback to vent out their frustration.

There might be still others, who are so into themselves that nothing worthwhile will come out from them.

In most cases you already know what you are good or bad at. But here you are trying to find out if there are blind spots. And how does the world perceive you. Perceptions may be true or not.

Apart from one-on-one feedback, you may also go for 360-degree surveys.

After completing all the above exercises, you would at last discover yourself.

Now, apply your lens on the type of organisation that matches your value system, and career aspirations. See what works in that type of organisation. You should then use or develop skills that are meaningful to achieve success in your organization.

I would also suggest that you take this opportunity to know yourself at a much deeper level.

Take time off to identify and rectify ego flaws that you might have. Well, everyone has one or more of them. But then, what is that predominant trait that defines your personality? Is it affecting you to a point where your growth is stunted? This exercise will make you more flexible and reduce your dependence on outside world in seeking happiness.

Some of these ego flavours as mentioned in ancient Hindu scriptures are -

1. **Superiority complex** - When you think you are superior to others around you. You may look down upon people and in worst cases, mistreat them. It might result in people hating you.

2. **Inferiority complex** - When you feel others are better than you. Here, you become shy and lack confidence. Others might stop believing in you.

3. **Guilt** - When you feel you have committed something wrong. This guilt will make you blame yourself and will devoid you from taking more ownership. People will stop enjoying your company.

4. **Victim** - When you start feeling that world is conspiring against you. This is most common and very difficult to get rid of. People hate to be in your company as you are regularly cribbing.

5. **Defensiveness** - When you start giving explanations for every wrong word said about you. You might say

things or do actions that reflect your defensive behaviour. In many cases, no one might even be talking about you, but you will start explaining, and then everyone will be confused why you are taking it on you. You are someone people can easily take advantage of.

6. **Aloofness** - A very natural transition state from victimhood. Very soon, you stop talking and get into a shell. People with suicidal tendencies are often aloof. People will stop talking to you as you demand so.

7. **Aggression** - When your frustrations build up from inside, you get into this mode, often harming yourself more than anybody else. People try to stay away from aggressive people. People are scared to give you feedback. It is highly likely that something bad will happen to you since you never listened to the warning signs. Then, you move into the victim category.

8. **Complaining** - When you keep grudging, it becomes a habit. This is another flavour of a victim who is more vocal. People want to run away from the ever - complaining types.

9. **Being Judgmental** - When you think you know everything. Superiority complex makes you judgmental and you stop enjoying the science of possibilities. You end up losing opportunities. You will never be able to make good use of resources that are readily available to you.

10. **Doership** - This is higher form of ego where you start believing that your accomplishments are because of you and you alone. Well, there are so many forces at work and perhaps it is time for you to be a bit humbler.

11. **Selfishness** - This is the most innate human trait. Larger good can be accomplished when you are able to give this up. There are different levels of selfishness. There are those who are selfish in each transaction, and then those who look at longer term. Each one has its disadvantage, but transaction wise selfish people are lonely, they can neither create nor maintain friendships.

All these flavours of ego are a major hassle in your growth, in team building, and in realizing numerous opportunities that organisations might be throwing at you and your team. Spend time to complete this flavour identification exercise. This will help you greatly at personal and professional level. And once you have identified it, become aware of this ego flavour whenever it surfaces. Just by being aware, you will be able to slowly get rid of it. The stronger the flavour of ego the more time it will take to get rid of it. But slowly and steadily, you will gain freedom from what is not your true self.

For your personal growth w.r.t. these ego flavours, get a copy of "Celebrating Life" by Rishi Nityapragya (Art of Living).

Chapter 4
Observe & Understand

नहि ज्ञानेन सदृशं

"There is nothing like knowledge in this world"

You have understood what are the different types of organisations. You have analyzed what you are good at, and more importantly what you love doing. Now, armed with these two sets of information, with full awareness, look at your organisation and start mapping your current organisation with the characteristic types of organisations you have learnt.

Eg: If you are someone who wants to make a mark in history with your innovation, type 2 (Risk Averse) and 6 (Resource Providers) are not for you.

Just look at your motivators, look at the type of company you are in and then understand what will work in this company.

I have a hunch that after reading this you might be thinking that I am asking you to switch jobs asap. Well, that is not my intention at all. I am just trying to bring out the reason, why you are not getting what you wish to get.

Think about this. If you want to learn merits of vegetarianism, you can't learn it in the company of a tiger.

Wake up! Either reset expectations or create a plan, and take ownership to execute it.

Let us move ahead in this pursuit to understand organisations. We may now use this excellent piece of wisdom to apply personal lens at the organisation level.

"यथा ब्रह्माण्डे तथा पिण्डे"

"As is the individual, so is the universe, as is the universe, so is the individual".

You would realize that it is really the aggregation of individual consciousness that makes the organisation consciousness. So, what all you experience with individuals, organisations go through the same.

With this principle in our mind, let us spend time in understanding ego flavours in context of organisation culture.

In last chapter we touched upon different flavours of ego from personal angle. You will be surprised to know that even organizations have certain ego types as part of their culture. Identify what flavour of consciousness is predominant in your organisation.

You might observe that there are certain organisations where members from Senior Management carry certain air, whereby it looks like they have come from another planet, and members working for them are lesser mortals.

If you have spent good many years in the industry and have experienced at least two or more organisations, you will realize that members who have spent a good amount of time in an organisation will continue to exhibit the organisation's cultural traits even after they move on to a different company. Funny thing is, that while this might be a normal behaviour in the organisation from where they caught this ego flavour, but in a new organisation everyone looks at them as someone who has come from a zoo.

Do look back and see if you are suffering from any such acquired ego flavour from the organisations that you worked for.

Another very common ego flavour that organisations have is complaining. Everyone would be talking ill of everyone else who is not present in this conversation. The real purpose is to tell that I am good at the cost of everyone else, who is portrayed as bad.

The problem with organisation level ego flavours is that if you do not participate you might feel that members stop trusting you. But there is always a middle path. If you are caught in such a situation, do not stop the person from criticizing. But then you should not participate either. So, you are not adding further negativity in the conversation. Now, try to slowly take this conversation to a positive direction.

It is very interesting to witness what happens when someone who does not have this ego flavour as part of his consciousness enters such an organisation.

One - He will keep it to himself and keep boiling from within.

Two - He might get into fights asking members not to speak ill. This will result in spoiling of his own relationship with colleagues for all the good intentions he might have.

Three - Worse still, he will start telling others what all was discussed in this conversation.

In the **first** case, he will get demotivated and frustrated.

In the **second** case, he will spoil his relationship with at least one person

In the **third** case, he will spoil multiple relationships.

I would again advice that if you are witnessing such an ego flavour in the organisation, just stay inert during these discussions. Do not participate and do not react. Just accept the situation and concentrate on your job.

दुर्जनं प्रथमं वन्दे सज्जनं तदनन्तरम् ।

"I first bow to the bad people for they are ruining themselves to teach me lesson of life. And then I bow to the wise for showing me the way."

I have been very fortunate to face some of the most politically inclined people who were very innovative at devising political strategies and creating political situations to suit their interests. And with a child-like innocence, I witnessed their plays in awe for I had no skill whatsoever to direct any such play myself.

In many such cases, I went beyond and tried to understand from the masters of this game. To my amazement, I did find a few, who were very vocal about how they play this game of chess.

The good thing is that some of these learnings were indeed applied by me to predict their next move. While it was very easy for me to realize that I cannot play such a game myself, but still this on job education helped me. It made be more aware and helped me to either accept the situation with humility or circumvent around it where I possibly could. I was also able to warn some of my friends and acquaintance in advance as to what will happen to them.

Corporate politics as a subject deserves a separate book which will indeed come from me in future. It will be filled with real life stories.

But for now, even though organisation culture is the subject of focus, some standard corporate political practices are being mentioned here so that you can appreciate the very subject of culture. The idea is for you to be aware so that you do not come in line of cross fire.

Some Common Political Practices:

1. Blame the past

When someone is given a new post, in order to set lower expectations, the person may start bringing out all the problems in the project/ program as if nothing good has ever been accomplished, and leadership has been kept in dark all the while. This is a typical tactic to buy time, and to set lower expectations so that once you accomplish something, you can exaggerate and get maximum benefit out of your achievement.

2. Create your comfort net

This mostly happens at senior management level. When people join an organisation, they would immediately identify peers who can make or break their job. And this club of convenience continues ever after. This coterie ensures that no one directly brings out any mistake of their group, and in return they demand similar favour.

The motto is 'United We Stay Safe'. The underlying emotion is **insecurity**.

Once this arrangement is made, you are the king of your own empire. The best part of this arrangement is that some personalities who are otherwise very aggressive will conduct themselves well with these peers.

We should always be gentle with our peers, but this arrangement means that many dependencies and problems faced by one's direct reports do not get resolved, eventually frustrating members and doing a greater harm to the organisation.

But an important thing for you to understand is that it is needed by certain individuals to find their feet in company. It is their insecurity rather than their limitation. So, if your dependencies are not getting resolved with a different group and your manager is not supportive, find alternate ways. Know that your manager will not be able to get it resolved. And that your manager will not allow you to fire at his peer for fear of a similar fire expected from the other side.

3. Kings use soldiers and loyalists to target able generals

If you are a general and wondering how some meek general or someone not worthy of picking arms is fighting with you, know that he is being provided all the ammunition by the king. It could be possibly happening because of king's insecurities. Or maybe the king wants to get his loyalist to pick up a position, and he feels that you might not fit in his game plan.

And one other possibility that exists is that it is a genuine case of someone on a suicide mission.

If it is a suicide case, just move out of his path, and allow him to blow up someone else.

But, if it is indeed not a suicide mission, identify the king behind the plot, and try to show your allegiance. If he does not blink, know that it is time for you to update your CV.

Chapter 5
What Will Not Work?

नात्यन्तं सरलैर्भाव्यं गत्वा पश्य वनस्थलीम् ।
छिद्यन्ते सरलास्तत्र कुब्जास्तिष्ठन्ति पादपाः ॥

"Do not be very upright in your dealings, as you would see in forest, the straight trees are cut down while the crooked ones are left standing."

Change cannot happen by doing the same thing in the same way over and over again. And then we wonder why we are not getting different results.

If you want to have lots of money, you can't work with safety nets around you (**Org type 2 - Risk Averse**). You have to go for companies driven by sheer revenue and margins (**Org type 12 - Urge for bigger revenue and profits**).

Start - up companies that originate out of passion (**Org type 11 - Passion for underlying product/ service**) are like love and you cannot bring in conditions of work life balance, or specific technology stacks, or fast money there. Rest assured, there will be learnings.

Safest bet for risk averse is resource providing firms (**Org type 6 - Resource providers**). Most service - based companies belong to this category.

Best insurance for your career is an ever- improving skill set and industry relevant experience.

In short term, you can have a different theme and still go for the company that does not match your long-term aspiration. I suggest that you do all those experiments when you are between 3 to 10 years of experience range **(Org type 7 - live by short term goals)**.

First three years are best spent on learnings, next 5 years in getting quick bucks. By now, you would hopefully understand your drivers (which keep changing:-) and then you get at your mid-term to long-term pursuits.

भद्रं भद्रं कृतं मौनं कोकिलैर्जलदागमे ।
दर्दूराः यत्र वक्तारः तत्र मौनं हि शोभते ॥

"On the onset of the rainy season, Cuckoo does not sing. Because where frogs croak, it is better to be silent"

If you have a dirty culture in your team with which you do not align, make attempts to improve/ raise your issue with higher ups for first 6 months. If it does not change in first 6 months, in all probability, it will not change for a good period of time.

There is no point continuing to raise your voice. If you see frogs always croaking around, and the cuckoo in you never gets a chance to exhibit competencies, **change your team now.** It is not worth spending years in frustration.

अङ्गारः शतधौतने मपलनत्वंन मञ्चुपत ।

"Coal does not lose its dirt even when it is washed a hundred times"

If you have joined a team with continuous past failures where your boss was directly handling the team or his loyalist handled it, and you have been added due to some pressure from organisation leadership, there are very high chances that your charisma, performance and hard work will not fetch you due appreciation.

The only way you can work this out is if you have a game plan to replace your boss.

However, if your boss had someone who handled the team and that person was not liked by the boss, even a little success will be much celebrated.

If you are given an award because of political reason, e.g. you have replaced someone who was disliked by your boss, don't be overexcited about it. In such a place, talent has no value. Enjoy till the party lasts!

If you are a leader and looking for talented people, looking for people with awards and certification will not help. Instead, look for people who have been doing challenging roles.

Another way to look for right talent is by asking someone in your organisation as to who can give you information on a particular subject.

Remember, talented people and good performers are those whom leaders meet in private, and political people are those who are talked about in public.

I do not mean that good people do not get rewarded, but just that awards do not guarantee either talent or performance.

In organisation types where client is the priority (**Org type 4 - customer centric**), you cannot succeed by making mark just by working magically with internal team.

Here, you have to become the face of the client. One word of praise from the client can work wonders for your career and one concern can devastate your career.

Also, job security lies with the client.

But beware as change of client means you start from scratch again. So, your core skills and interpersonal qualities are still the most important assets in such type of job.

Certifications can help create buzz, certifications can help members who have forgotten to learn from life, certifications can help the marketing department, but certifications will not work in creating a culture of learning.

Same applies to **surveys** and **industry awards/ recognitions**. If favourable survey results come naturally during work, and if awards are received without extensive preparation such as studying the criteria and specifically preparing for them, they can provide valuable insights. However, planned and rehearsed surveys and awards are not reliable for making decisions.

So, certifications are no criteria, awards are no criteria, and surveys are no criteria in judging the best.

I don't mean to undermine them. They do tell us that a certain level of maturity has been reached. The company has spent some time in ensuring that some of its limitations have been overcome, and some basic hygiene is maintained.

If you have to guess whether a company has a good culture, and it is a case where you do not have any impartial references, surveys, certifications and awards do come handy.

They are like passing percentage in school exams. If you can't conduct your own entrance exam, you might want to consider them as a criterion. But for you to really excel, do not go by certificates, awards and surveys.

If you find companies spending more and more time in award preparations and surveys, it is not a good use of organisation resources. They are missing on strong fundamentals and covering it up with these.

But here are a few exceptions. If you have young students, awards and certifications do indicate their learnings. As they grow old, life gives them many more practical lessons and those theory marks don't matter anymore.

Same applies to organisations. If it is a new organisation trying to find feet in this world, you might want to check on some of these criteria. But as it grows, these measures only mean more bureaucracy.

Isn't it funny that no investment bank likes to add process overheads like CMMI but most service companies that support these banks exhibit these certifications.

Remember, a genius has neither time nor energy to get entangled in processes.

For full blossoming of a company, it has to help its members break free.

When you think deep, you understand that processes are also very important, but they should not kill innovation. And then, you need to keep genius of your company beyond all processes. Give them their breathing space, and you will see how they bring exponential growth for your organisation.

Chapter 6
What Will Work?

सिंहवत्सर्ववेगेन पतन्त्यर्थे किलार्थिनः ॥

"Those who intend to get work done, cast themselves on the task with all possible speed, like a lion"

Breathing space is absolutely critical for any individual to realize his full potential. And this very freedom granted to an individual will take the organisation to next level of maturity. I am not talking about the stretches and times where one has to give his 200% percent when nearing the goal line. That is normal in any industry. But your day job should only keep you 80% busy for the larger part of the year.

Organisation initiatives that aim to bring a change in culture should be run like how an artist paints his canvas. Sometimes he stays awake in night to paint, sometimes he has to go to an ice cave to get his motivation, sometimes he needs to drink to death to reach certain madness where it brings out a master piece.

Setting hard bound processes around initiatives and putting Service level agreements (SLAs) and Key Result Areas (KRAs) is like keeping a knife on the neck of a golden egg laying duck. Under the threat of sword, only fanaticism can be promoted, spirituality grows by letting go.

What works is when a person is given his 20% time to paint the canvas. Now, that 20% could be an opportunity for him to do consulting, or learn artificial intelligence, or create a white paper on project management practice, or write a book. But where each of this is put as an expectation, brilliance will never be achieved.

Now, critics will come and say that there are so many people who will simply sleep their way during that 20% offered leisure time. The answer to this is that these individuals will not grow, and it will only bring stability to your company. We need all kinds of people to run an organisation. At the end of the day, it should really be an individual's call. May be sleep is what the individual needs most at the moment.

We just learnt that some spare time is needed for you to grow, and for an organisation to grow. And that time should not be governed by SLAs and KRAs. Check if your dream organisation provides that.

I have been talking about organisation culture and the need for you to pick the right kind of organisation. But let me give you an electric shock here. If given a choice between a good organisation and a good boss, my recommendation is to choose the good boss. **It will work.** Let us understand why I say so.

Organisations with any kind of culture will always have certain level of politics. This politics will keep growing as you move up the ladder. If your manager acts as a comfortable condo unit that provides the right environment for you to blossom even when it is snowing outside, what else do you need? You can do miracles under such a roof.

There are tons of examples where the whole team moved with the manager. Not only it is the safety net, it also comes with strong growth opportunities. And then it provides you with the right guidance that is so very much needed to grow in this highly competitive corporate world.

Mentor is someone who works like magic in the corporate world. We have seen numerous examples where people grew when they got the right mentor. It is like a full structure of same set of people moving together bound by a common mentor, growing together as time passes. If you have a mentor, not only do you get the right advice, he will also have you in his mind as a loyal comrade and will help you in bagging that sought after position.

Relationships take time to develop. You save on all the time you have to spend in fighting or understanding the working style, or needing to adapt to a person's style. It is such a pain that many a times you have to study body language to find out that a no is actually a yes. And then there are times when you keep wondering how the manager will think if you do A vs B, or what explanations to come up with, when someone complains against you to your boss.

All this cycle gets reduced drastically if you work with the same manager, and the same team. It is a win-win for both the boss and the team.

Another way to understand this is that a known enemy is better than an unknown friend. And here you are getting a choice between a known friend and an unknown "who knows friend or enemy". I am not asking you to stop experimenting with life. I am just saying that if the options are not too enticing, go with the reliable boss.

Short term gains will work with any organisation as long as you are clear as to what you are targeting and you have no reason to doubt whether the organisation will provide you what it has promised in a short term.

Eg: If a startup is offering you loads of money (**Org type 7 - live by short term goals or 11 - driven out of passion for the underlying product/ service**), and you are a year away from your kind of job, and need some fun on the way, go for it.

Now, let us talk about things that will work in every organisation. These are the basic ground rules that an employee should know lest he should be surprised why things did not work out.

These are the fourteen rules that you should learn by heart. And then take time to develop the underlying skills needed, so that you start exhibiting these in your thoughts and actions.

1. Develop deep knowledge in your core skill.

Be it design for an architect, material knowledge for a civil engineer, Java or Python language for a software programmer, so on and so forth, you have to master the basics. You cannot think of growth unless and until you are true to the basic skill for which you are being paid.

We had this programmer with such a charming personality that he would get along with client stakeholders so well that everyone treated him with a lot of respect.

One of those clients with whom he had worked on a long assignment was setting up a new team. We went to the client proposing his name assuming that it will be a hit. To our surprise, the client turned the proposal down asking not to impose him.

We got surprised yet again when we took his name to another client with whom he had worked in the past. He seemed to be a celebrated member in that team where client would talk to him more than anyone else. This gentleman also turned him down saying that the guy had poor technical skills.

With this, we went back and studied the work that he had delivered. We realized that his part of system had more defects than any other sub-system. We all thought these were not the defects introduced by him because it never got escalated and we all had relatively limited understanding of the project delivered.

Possibly, this is where his soft skills had helped him. He could get away by convincing the client, the project manager, and his boss that this was normal and not due to his mistakes. But then, we should understand that it is only a matter of time before those who are missing on basic skills, get caught. And then we wonder that after such a stellar performance why is someone not getting a job.

Remember, no wonder how pleasant you are at talking, no one has time to clean the garbage created by you.

2. Ability to understand your personality, and personality of people around you.

Do you remember what we discussed in chapter 3? If your stakeholder lacks patience, you can't bombard him with all the details of the world. It is suicidal to do so.

There was this hard - core techie who would spend day and night in doing perfect job. He was quite celebrated in multiple projects that he worked on. But he had a weakness - speaking his mind out.

Now what happens when such a person comes in contact with a stakeholder who has limited understanding of technology, and on top of that, hates details.

This guy would keep talking about the technology and its limitations, while the other person just wanted a crisp yes or no.

It was very shocking to see that this techie was moved out from this project by the stakeholder. Well, he surely got into another great project. But the point is that business suffered because neither this techie understood personality of his stakeholder, and then the stakeholder was equally naive in understanding this techie's style. And the result is everyone's loss.

But then, how would you know what is the other person's communication style? Well, if you have a long relationship with him, you will learn. But life seldom gives you so much time, especially when you are working with someone who is sitting somewhere much up in the ladder. Here, the idea of mastering 1 min talk is important so that you can create an impression with whatever time destiny offers you with someone influential.

You should start now to develop that skill of observing and finding the personality style of your stakeholders.

3. Communication skills (verbal as well as written) along with right sense of timing, and ability to filter the message.

Many people mistake language expertise with communication. If you are good in a language, it will help you. But then, you have to be precise. You should also be able to bring out the right tone, whether in verbal or written communication. And then you should know what to say in order to get the expected result from a conversation. Your purpose from conversations should not be to tell what you know. It should also not be to vent out your emotions. The aim for any discussion is to achieve what you want from that conversation. Always keep the result in your mind when you carry a formal conversation.

There was a very hard working and committed person in a service company who used to toil day and night. But he never got appreciated. Let us call him Mr X. The problem was that there were multiple client stakeholders giving him work on a regular basis. While he tried his best, it was impossible to satisfy all of them.

These client stakeholders started complaining about him to their senior. This was when things started getting really difficult for him.

With all these complaints, the senior client stakeholder sent a nasty mail to him asking for reasons for delay in task completion.

Mr X got emotional and responded saying that he has been working day and night. He gave a lot of information in a directionless manner. This made the senior stakeholder even more furious.

Mr X decided to resign and went to his manager. The manager knew that Mr X was well skilled and very committed.

It did not take much time for him to understand the situation. He explained that it was lack of prioritization, and bad communication.

A precise mail was hence sent explaining different work items being assigned by different stakeholders, along with the task complexity, schedule and effort estimates.

The mail response also included a suggestion requesting to route the work via one point of contact so that priorities could be decided optimally between the client stakeholders.

With this mail, things became so clear for everyone that no further discussion on the topic was deemed necessary. And guess what, the very next week, he received his first appreciation from the client.

Here, we just turned an angry client into an admirer. Before this communication, Mr. X was on the verge of losing this job. But now he started getting appreciation for the very same work.

If all of us could communicate well, I am sure it would mean so many more appreciations and a healthy and happy work environment. Every communication would then become a reason for the sender and the receiver to smile. This will go a long way to make the entire world a lot more simple, happy and worthy of living.

I am now convinced that communication is the single most important skill apart from the core. It is useful in whatever we do. **Develop it now!**

4. Understanding preferences of your boss and people around you.

Remember knowing people's personality type is one time activity but preferences change over a period of time. For someone struggling with a production outage or someone who has just been thrashed by his boss for operations, you can't really go and give a brilliant next generation solution that will take 6 months to develop. Wake up my dear, and understand what is the need of the hour.

I recall that time when for a critical project that had major operational issues, concerned manager kept trying to explain to his boss that it requires major platform improvement. He was right. The platform was not in a state where it could embrace any new feature. But then, the stakeholder was so bugged up by the daily issues that he wanted his manager to take up a frontal role in managing them. Stakeholder wanted a pain killer and not a prescription for long term medication to fix the underlying disease. The setup was one that did not support the manager to pick up day to day operations efficiently. But then, his repeated pleas to his boss to redo the platform felt like as if the guy is running from the operations and talking about something not related to the agenda. It was only natural that he would soon be shunted out. Did moving him solve the boss's problem? No! But the guy lost it anyways.

If you are in such a situation where strategic work is not a priority and operations has challenges that are beyond you, I would suggest you look out for another job. Because most probably, someone higher up is already finding a more viable replacement. Better preempt it. Another way to look at it is to understand what is the priority for your boss. You should just concentrate on that priority. Do talk about the future path, but do not spend too much time on it. Don't over emphasize something that the other person is not even interested in listening to.

5. Honesty is still the best policy, but timing matters.

There is no denying that truth ultimately comes out. So, no point in hiding it. In fact, if you do not speak it, someone else will. And that will mean breach of trust. Without trust, no relationship can survive.

So, do tell the truth, but ensure that you do not tell at a time when the person is in a bad mood. Your truth can take him to a hospital bed, or move you out of the organisation. Having said that do not delay beyond a few days.

6. No washing dirty linen in public.

Those public fights can either entertain people at your cost, or spoil your reputation. They can - not produce any good result for you.

Some of the reasons why you may want to fight in front of everyone:

- I want to expose the person in front of everyone.
- I am only responding to an allegation made about me. If I don't, people will assume that I am guilty.
- I get too angry and do not realize that everyone is watching.
- I don't want to wait for resolution. I want to end it right now.

Do think of a time when you saw people fighting in public. I am sure their reason to fight would be one of the above. Recall what was your reaction on seeing them fight.

No matter what is your rationale for doing it, remember that it will never benefit you.

7. If you must fight, fight with speech and not with pen.

A harsh word spoken either hurts once or a few times, but something put on record is like preserving a live deadly virus. It will keep reminding the person and have him relive the pain every moment. And you will have an enemy for life.

There was this extremely hard working and effective person who had some ugly fights with one of the influential peers. In the heat of moment, she wrote a really nasty mail explaining why she thinks that the person is doing harm to the company and does not deserve this position. Times changed, and this peer became a golden eyed boy for the higher ups.

While this hard - working person tried her best to find truce, and apologized multiple times, the other person kept this mail close to his heart. And there was a time when an important decision around the person's exit had to be made. The mail ensured that the wound was never healed, and hence closed the doors of the company on her.

8. Don't give direct feedback.

Feedback is a very important tool. It helps you by bringing to your attention some hard facts that you might be missing. It also helps you to realize what is the perception people have about you.

If you care for someone you will be tempted to give a feed-back.

My advice is to give it if the other person has asked for it. Give it based on his maturity, and your relationship with him.

Try to sandwich constructive feedback by putting it between two strengths. That would make it much more effective and you might just save a relationship that could have got disrupted by the bitterness of truth.

 There was this magician, who would use his magic wand to solve all problems.

This person charmed his new boss in the new, challenging job. Everything seemed to be going perfect as he had been able to prove himself in first few months itself.

And then, one fine day, over the drinks, his boss asked him what he felt about his fellow leads. The person kept giving nice to hear statements. But the boss insisted to hear it straight from the heart.

He thought that he owes to his boss nothing but truth. And he started... He talked how negative the whole environment is. And the fact that whenever a task is assigned, each leader first thinks whom they will blame if there is a failure. It typically means that the team has to live under this constant fear of failure. How can such a team ever succeed? Now, the boss asked him to write to all leads saying the same. Thankfully, he did not do that. But whatever he said was good enough to bring him down. God knows if the boss told the same to the leads or not, but the magician was soon left isolated by all other leads, and he was soon shown the exit door by the boss.

I don't intend to discourage you from speaking truth. But bitter truth can either lead you to great success, or harm you with your job. To play safe, first understand the environment.

9. Use more data and less emotions.

Data is your best friend. With data you can tell the most unpleasant truth without getting personally involved. Emotions only bring hatred in conversations. Whenever, emotions get high on you, take deep breaths and come back to the data points.

I have seen countless examples where data saved the day. I hardly see people making full use of data available to them. Look around, and you will find the best ammunition lost in your reports that you can use to get successful.

I am not undermining the importance of emotions. But then emotions should be channelized. Preserve them for a time when using them will benefit you. Using emotions for success requires lot of craftsmanship, but data is an easy -to- use tool.

10. Keep showing value at regular intervals.

People have short memories. Instead of giving 10 great things at the same time, if you can space them at regular intervals, people will value it more. And they will continue to value your worth.

Enthusiasm is an enemy when it comes to timing your value adds. In the heat of moment, you tell what all you are working on, and then expectations get built. Also, once you have exhausted yourself, you need more time to come up with the next set. But then expectations have been set and no matter how hard you work; you will never be able to impress further. So, plan things in a way that it is not overwhelming for you. Keep working in the background and bring it to the surface at the right time.

11. Do not burn bridges even if you have to leave an organisation.

This world is a small place. Today's foes can become tomorrow's friends. Why poison your future to satisfy a momentary urge to spit venom at someone?

There was this very emotional person who had multiple small fights with his manager. He sided with the manager's colleague in proving him wrong multiple times. And when he could not bear any more, he decided to quit. He moved laterally into a different project with a different boss. And once his new role was sealed, he thought of getting even with his old boss. He went out and spit whatever venom he had accumulated all these years. Guess what? Things did not work out in the new role and he had to now go back to the same team. His earlier manager had now grown one level above. He now found that whatever project he worked on and whatever success he achieved, he was not getting any reward or recognition for it. He kept trying hard, kept moving between teams but the past experience with the leader ensured that he never got any respite. Finally, he had to quit the organisation. If you ask him today whether that outburst was worth it, he will surely say no. If you must part ways, move out with grace.

12. Don't forget but do forgive.

It is stupid to not learn from past. And so, you should never forget. But to not forgive is even more stupid. Forgiveness not only opens up a future possibility but helps you feel better. The weight of carrying thousand revenges is not worth. Throw it away.

13. Be a good negotiator.

Negotiation skills help you everywhere. Let us say you are working out a sales negotiation for some service with your client. Your client has set some limit internally beyond which he will not go. He will not reveal that limit to you. You too have a certain limit that has been set for you by your leadership, below which you can't sell. I am sure you don't want to reveal it either. The key is to know the other person's limit and not to tell yours. And that becomes basis of sales negotiation.

How do you know it? How do shopkeepers know that you are really interested in something? Body language is a great tool. Your pupils expand with excitement when you see something you long for. And then the shopkeeper puts up an exorbitant price. But you still buy it.

There are strategies to even play with that preset limit. Play with the ego. See which ego flavour is rampant in the other person.

The good thing is that negotiation skills can be learnt from anywhere. You can go to a shopping store and start practicing it. The same skill can very well be applied when you set expectations with your boss, when you are being given a fairly aggressive goal. Remember, it is the expectations that determine whether a task was successful or not. So, set it to your advantage.

14. Always introspect and retrospect.

Life is a great coach. For those who look within, their growth is guaranteed. No book or course can give this invaluable learning than your own mind when turned inwards.

Chapter 7
Time Management

न ही कश्चित् विजानाति किं कस्य श्वो भविष्यति।
अतः श्वः करणीयानि कुर्यादद्यैव बुद्धिमान्॥

"No one knows what is going to happen tomorrow. So doing all of tomorrow's task today is a signature of wise."

Time Management as a subject does not have to necessarily align with type of organisation culture. But it is such an important topic that it cannot be skipped here. There are some particular types of organisations where growth can happen only if you are very good at it. Else, you will not succeed. Worse, it will affect your health.

Let us start with a question - What is it that organisation expects from you w.r.t. time?

Forget about all wonderful things like innovation, value, quality, motivation, coaching skills etc. and for now just think about time and how you manage that.

Ultimately, it boils down to three things that matter for organisation leadership, in context of time:

1. It expects you to do more in less time.

2. It expects you to spend more time at work.

3. It expects you to do what really matters for business.

Let us dissect each of these.

1 - Do more in less time.

Organisations 1,4,5,7,9,11 would expect this. They need smart people to turn around things very quickly.

But how do you do more in less time?

a) You need to be very skilled to accomplish this. What skills would you need here?

- You should have a background in this domain and technology.
- You need to know ways of getting things done in this organization. For this, you need to have a strong network.

b) You need to be hollow and empty. If you are filled with so much stuff in your mind, you will never be able to give 100% to the work. For this, you should have a good personal life, and you should be in good health. I strongly recommend practices of Pranayama and Meditation to achieve this.

2 - Spend more time at work

Organizations 5,9,11 and 12 might expect you to do this. Others may compel you to spend long hours if the culture is dipped in bureaucracy. You would be amazed that even some of the most admired organisations have this dirt of bureaucracy in specific regional offices. They are doing well because they have an IP where a few bright people had brought in some innovation. Or because of relationships where the client is tolerating this because of pressure being exerted from the top.

3 - Do what matters to the business

The first two points discussed have nothing to do with the topic of time management. This third point is what drives it.

Any good organisation would want you to concentrate on what matters to the business. And prioritization is the key to effective time management.

Now that you understand what is time management and what is not, we delve into effective ways of prioritizing our tasks.

We had those good old days (say a few hundred years back) when people used to have limited set of tasks. There were very few distractions. So, if someone came with urgency you would pick the new task and drop what you were doing. Or say no and continue doing what you were doing. Life happened in black and white. You never had to keep track of tasks. Call it **Method 1**.

Then came the industrialization, era of machines. Now, people starting maintaining time tables and would do everything by the script. This generation was very rule book oriented. Everything would follow the rule book. While it helped doing a greater number of tasks, we lost our spontaneity. We could no longer pick important tasks that came unplanned because our time table did not agree to it. Call it **Method 2**.

Then came a time when people understood the need to implement the famous four quadrants.

In this approach, you have one axis for important and not important work, and another for urgent and not urgent tasks. This gives you four quadrants and you start putting items under them. You put everything that you have in your mind. And keep updating the list. And then you decide the order to pick work items from the list.

Logically speaking, this sounds great and should ideally work. You are actively aware of what is coming your way and keep putting into four quadrants and hence do not waste any time. You have a sense of direction and keep growing. Call it **Method 3**.

To understand the above strategies, and specially the last approach (Method 3) in detail, do read the two books - "the 7 habits of highly effective people" and "First Things First" by Stephen Covey.

From my experience, third one helps you prioritize but then it comes with a big challenge. It plays on your mind. Every day you end up looking at what you have achieved, and then you look at the long laundry list, and collapse. Every minute you are thinking about how to squeeze things in. And that gives you stress, lot of stress.

What is the way out? The best approach our generation learnt is not acceptable to our mind.

I suggest that you write the most important tasks (not all-important tasks). And then pick just 1-2 for the day that are most urgent. This is the only pick I have from method 3. Of course, you should be aware of the four quadrants and then your mind will do the rest sub consciously.

If something comes your way that is far more important and urgent, you will pick it up by default. If you forget it, most probably it is not worth remembering. There are many things that are not worthy of your time. Let time pass by and they will get resolved on their own.

You also pick a few lines from the method 2. For tasks with end date/ time, do put some entries in your calendar or set some reminders here and there. But then ensure that your calendar is at least half empty. That way, you get the best of method 1 as well.

Try this out. This combination of the three methods helps you stay put on your path. It helps you achieve hard deadlines too. And then it gives you the agility to pick things as they come. The best part is that this approach is stress free.

Chapter 8
Some Questions

गतशोकं न कुर्वीत भविष्यं नैव चिन्तयेत्
वर्तमानेषु कार्येषु वर्तयन्ति विचक्षनः

"There is no point in worrying about past or about future. A smart and intelligent person thinks and works only about present"

Here is a list of questions in case you have any doubts left after reading through last 6 chapters. You may keep it handy so that you can refer to it whenever you get puzzled as to why things are happening a particular way in your organisation.

❋ **I see that my career growth is stunted. What should I do?**

☑ You need to go through the first two chapters.

Post that, spend some time to write down your definition of career growth and whether your organization is capable of providing that.

We will go through the career document in chapter 10 which is an excellent tool for career growth.

Identify what skills are needed for the position that you are eyeing on. Do a quick check on whether you have the required skill set. If you have the required skill set, are you exhibiting those at any forum? In case you do not have the required skill set, you will need to develop that to achieve this growth. And once you have done all the above, identify what kind of support you need from management. Talk to them and convince them that this support will be a win-win.

Two things to understand here:

One, if you are learning, it does mean growth. It is just that the actual jump to next level happens, when necessary, skill and experience is accumulated.

Two, give 6 months to the organisation and see if things are going in right direction. Post that, one and a half year should be the maximum time by when you should have made measurable progress from a long -term perspective. Remember, these two durations - 6 months and 1.5 years.

❈ I see someone without any skills getting promoted while I am still at the same place. What should I do?

☑ Find out if he is doing something that is not known to you. Also, what might not be important to you might be a must have for the next level. Example - in service industry members feel that client praise is all that you need for growth. While your compensation and appreciation might have direct relation with that, but line management and internal processes are also needed for project sustenance.

If you have been shying away from doing that, possibly that is the reason why your growth is stunted.

While this is one possibility, there may still be other things at play that neither books will teach you nor will management tell you openly.

Please read the underwritten carefully so that you understand what happens behind the scene.

Your growth is highly dependent on how comfortable leadership is with you. As you move up the ladder, you will observe that leaders want brilliant people to be two levels below them so that they do not pose any direct threat. These brilliant people are very much needed to run operations, and to grow the organisation. But one level down are often members who are loyal and whose skills don't go beyond the leader.

So, threat and loyalty are two important factors. Do understand how these two play out in your case. And understand management's point of view before deciding your next move.

※ **I performed great in my project but did not get any reward, while that person got promoted even when**

his project failed to launch. Why did this happen to me?

☑ Ironically, growth and appreciation are also dependent on your criticality to the organisation and project in hand. So, you have to see where you are placed in context of future opportunities. It will only be fair to say that typically 80% of managers consider criticality of a person a bigger factor compared to actual performance while deciding appraisal grades, compensation, bonus, or promotion.

✻ I don't like the work I am doing. Should I switch my job?

☑ Strangely, Mahatma Gandhi's quotes are still applicable in modern times and in context of corporate world.

One - think of work as worship. You can't dislike your religion and still practice it.

Two - Gandhi's explanation of "**Satyagrah**" was so deep. He would say that first follow the current process with full dedication. This is what your employer or leadership or government has asked you to do. And only once you have experienced and are convinced it is not the right thing or right way, then do a "**satya ka agrah**" insistence on truth. Now, think about it from corporate perspective.

Whatever work you are doing, worship it. Either worship it or do not do it at the first place.

Once you are comfortable with the work, and that typically happens when you have spent some good amount of time in doing/ repeating it, you can then decide if there is a better way to do it. Or you can decide whether it should not be done at all.

Tell your management what you think, and also why you think that way. Don't just go with problem. You have to provide solution as well. And that solution has to be properly thought around. You have to be ready for any possible question that comes your way.

And if after all this, they still don't listen, find a better place where people listen to you.

✵ I have an offer of 40% hike from another company. Should I take it?

☑ You will always find a job that is more paying. But remember it should not shorten your life. At the end of day, the purpose of life is to be happy and to stay a little longer in this world.

If it is hurting you so much, talk to your management. If they provide some correction, take it. If they don't listen at all, switch. But don't switch jobs for small hikes.

* **I love to innovate and build competency. I have been waiting for an opportunity to do something worthwhile but nothing is happening. What should I do?**

☑ Go back to chapter 2 and see what is the kind of company you are working for. Also, see if your job is giving you time to think. If not, pack up and move.

* **My company keeps promising me great opportunities but never fulfils it. What should I do?**

☑ Find out if they have a valid reason. Sometimes you lack the skills that are necessary for your growth. You will not get it anywhere else also.

But then, do not expect management lessons from primary school. See if you are at the right place.

※ **My friends are starting a new venture. Should I join them?**

☑ Understand from them what is the business model. Whatever it be, history says there are 90% chances that it will fail. Count your savings, and see if you are at a point in your career where you can easily get the job again.

※ **In these turbulent times, is it safe to switch jobs?**

☑ Depends on your risk appetite. As long as you have some savings, and you feel you have decent skills to keep you afloat, you can move.

※ **My company finds mention in magazines but I do not see anything special about it.**

☑ Don't go by magazines. Personal experience is always better than any magazine review. Through preparation, money and contacts, anyone can ensure an entry into some column or the other.

※ **I keep complaining to my manager about this team which keeps failing us on our dependencies. But he says that I need to find a way out. I am scared as I have no control over this other team. What do I do?**

☑ Try to subtly pass on message to other influencers or stakeholders about the challenges with the other team. But be ready with your resume. More often than not, a manager who cannot help you in resolving dependencies and does not even try to resolve it, will not stand by you if project fails. Either you work those dependencies out yourself, or move out from there.

* **My colleague is very jealous of me and keeps abusing me in public. My manager does not do anything about it though I have taken this team to high maturity level through months of hard work. Why is this colleague acting this way and why my manager is not doing anything about it?**

☑ Is your manager fearing that you will take his position or has ego hassles with you? Abusing is an HR issue. If manager is not acting, chances are that it is happening with his approval. If you have good contacts and are the right person for the job, get the duo out and take your boss' position. If you can't do that, move out quietly. For sure, such duo will ultimately fail. But if you keep suffering, they will keep taking credit for your success and you will keep getting abused.

* **I spent lot of time in creating POC out of this amazing idea. But I do not have support to create**

product offering out of it. Why management is not able to realize its potential?

☑ It could be due to two reasons.

One - you are expecting it from a company whose business model has nothing to do with IP creation. It is one thing to talk about IP creation as marketing stunt, and another thing to realize it.

Two - your idea might not actually make business sense.

※ **I hear lot of employees got hikes when they threatened to leave the organisation. I feel I am paid pennies and am a victim just because I don't like to bargain. What should I do?**

☑ Talk to management and get your hike if you really think that works. Don't become a victim. Move ahead and do it. But also remember, if you threaten with resignation for money, then there is a probability that you will lose trust of senior management. Instead, talk about your genuine concern and if you are applicable, it will be taken care. But then, if you really feel there is a big difference and it is not working out, who is stopping you from moving to another place? Whatever be the case, do not hide behind your ego flavour as it will only hurt you more.

※ **I talked about my latest idea and delivery in team meeting. To this, my manager gave my example in front of the whole team as to how we should work. But strangely, from then on, my friends stopped including me in our usual chat sessions or during coffee breaks. I feel very sad and not sure what is happening. What could have gone wrong?**

☑ My dear friend, your boss has given you one appreciation and taken away your support structure in return. Impress your bosses and juniors but not your peers. There is one school of thought which says that awards bring jealousy and make work environment bad. I am not against awards, but then, be humble in front of peers. And managers should never make comparisons in public. Examples should be given, and awards can also be given in public but without, comparing with others.

※ **Do we really have any organisation that has empathy embedded in its culture? How to find that while during job search?**

☑ Empathy is a loosely used term. Empathy is normally understood as something where you are able to feel the same way the other person is feeling. I believe this is very hard for any individual to accomplish. Even if you can imagine all the conditions that person is going through, each one of us have been built differently. So, to completely feel the same way is almost impossible. You can at most be sympathetic. And having basic sensitivity and sympathy towards fellow employee is very important. Each one of us have gone through some tough times in our lives. How your professional family supports you can make or break you at that moment. Organisations either have it or not. It might not depend on the type of organisation that we discussed before. For this again, you should talk to individuals who have worked in the organisations in the past or read about their leaders at senior level. If they have been sympathetic, it would reflect in the company's culture.

※ **While presenting my work, should I worry about the sheer presentation side of it? Or I should just concentrate on the core content?**

☑ It depends on your industry and kind of job you are in. If you are an architect, strong fundamentals matter the most. Eg: Light, air circulation, direction, etc. are the core of an architect's work. But then, if you do not make it presentable with right material, people would not get tempted to live in the house. If I have to give a magic percentage, I would say the focus should be 80% on core and 20% on presentation. But then, it depends.

Another way to look at it is based on who is consuming the content of your work. If the person understands the subject, he will focus on the meat of the work, but if he is naive, he will only worry about the look and feel of it. It is like you presenting future strategy of your company to the investors. If they are intelligent enough, they will solely look at the plan and data supporting the plan. But for those who have limitations of the brain, they will keep looking at your presentation - colours and pictures and fonts of it. Even if you have a great story, and excellent audience, I would still suggest to spend some time to ensure that the bad presentation does not irritate them.

Here is a story to explain.

Once Lord Krishna had a meeting planned with prince Duryodhana. Duryodhana was the eldest son of king Dhritarashtra. Duryodhana represented evil, and someone who was too involved in worldly pleasures. Lord Krishna was spending lot of time on his make - up. He chose the best of clothes, the finest of jewellery and had his hair curled to make him look really royal and handsome. His support staff got very puzzled. Why is God himself spending so much time in presentation when he was the best amongst men of all times?

They asked him why and that too for a person as lowly as Duryodhana?

To this Krishna said, "Your answer is in the question. Someone as stupid as Duryodhana does not understand that the divinity within the human form should be the subject of interest. His small mind gets stuck with the ornaments and looks.

And so, to get something from him, I need to work on what seems so unnecessary to you. If I were to meet Devas and Rishis and Gopis, I will not spend any time on this makeup, for they realize the divinity and would not waste time to look at the surface."

I hope you have got the answer. Some bit of clean presentation is needed for all cases. But then, depending on the client and your core job, you might have to adjust where you spend your time.

Chapter 9
Notes for Senior Leadership

आ नो भद्राः क्रतवो यन्तु विश्वतः ।

"Let noble thoughts come to me from all directions"

There are many common leadership quotes that go around in corporate world. They are so common and simple that leaders often miss them while they keep searching for more complex solutions, and attend to resplendent behavioural lessons. This chapter lists these 'must follow' common rules. My humble advice is not to ignore them. These are the things that are extremely important and are often seen missing in organisations.

❖ Lead By Example.

If you are asking your management team to conduct skip levels, please do so yourself first.

If you want people to be good listeners, control your temptation to cut people while they are speaking.

If you want an open culture, stop shooting the messengers.

How many sales heads actually win any sales deal? If they do not have experience in handling client, how can they expect their leads to do the same? And more importantly how do they know their leads are doing a good job?

The problem often seen with leadership is that they have no experience in doing things they dictate to their leads. Now this means that whatever targets are negotiated with their leads, become definition of success. Hence, a successful executive becomes someone who negotiates well, not necessarily who gets business in difficult situations.

First problem is that some people in leadership positions were poor performers in their past. Second problem is that they judge people who are more skilled than them and define priorities for them. This means that the actual tasks that get business revenue and profits suffer due to wrong priorities set by them.

There is this famous proverb by Chinese philosopher Confucius: "To know that we know what we know, and that we do not know what we do not know, that is true knowledge".

Be honest to yourself in what you know and what you do not know. And then see what you want to preach, what you want to exhibit by your actions, and what you want to really measure.

❖ Do not lose touch with ground.

Hierarchy helps in two ways. One, it saves your time. Two, it makes your team more accountable. It makes them believe that you have faith in them. This ensures that they take complete ownership and strive hard to succeed.

But then, you should not turn blind eye to your leads' mistakes. It is your right and your duty to not lose touch with ground. Otherwise, the middle layers might obstruct your view of ground reality.

Let us try to understand why you do not like to hear or act on complaints about your direct reports.

Is it because your credibility is at stake since you hired them?

Or is it because you fear becoming a bad guy as your direct report will reveal that the disliked policies are actually being run on your instructions? And he is taking the blame so that your reputation does not suffer?

Or is it because you feel that you have to still keep the same people even if they are faltering since the whole process of getting a better person is too much work for you?

My answer to all these is that it is still better to know the truth even if it means one of the above. People are smart enough to make out whose policy it is anyways. If not anything else, it will make people feel that you at least care to hear, even if you do not take action. Also, it will caution your star leads that they are not above the business. And then, they will be more careful.

❖ Be open to feedback.

As we move up the ladder, we become too arrogant to accept feedback. In fact, if someone says a word against us or our policies, we boil in anger. Worse, we take it so much to our ego that we decide to shoot the messenger. There are so many of them out there, whose reactions are too violent, as if telling the world not to say anything that requires them to act otherwise there will be repercussions. And a natural corollary is that such people very soon lose touch with ground.

When you receive feedback, you are always within your right not to implement the suggestion or change. Just accept as it comes and move ahead. Once you have patience to hear, you will be amazed to realize that some of the things marked as improvement are basic etiquettes and it will not cost you a fortune to implement them.

❖ Do not impose policies purely based on your personal experience and priority in life.

While Empathy is a great virtue, don't mistake your feelings with what others are feeling. If you can't empathize, sympathy is a better value to pursue. You feel that your team is dying for a party if you are a party person. You should understand that there are those people also in this world who are desperate to catch some sleep or those for whom number one priority in life is to give some quality time to their family. For them party is like stretching work beyond office hours.

You could as well be someone who loves solitude and would impose solitary confinement on your team members assuming they love privacy.

My only advice to you is not to impose your thoughts on others. Ask them what they want.

❖ Treat people with respect.

Each position is temporary in this world. If you get hurt when you fall, if your blood is as red as others, and if you know that you will have to leave this body one day, then why let your arrogance take over your senses? If power and position intoxicate you, and you insult people, remember, all the suffering that you are causing to others will come back to you once you retire.

Such people suffer the most once this position of power goes away from them. A quick look at retired life of such people will surely bring a change in your attitude. If you are smart, then feel happy about it. Why do you want to insult someone because he is not as smart as you? And what will happen to you if the other person is smarter than you? Are you ready to hear the same dirty words from him?

Live and let live.

❖ Do not forget your team when you grow in your career.

These are the people who have helped you grow. Who knows you might need them some day. And even if that does not happen, word of mouth spreads and those who forget their team ultimately find that no one wants to work for them.

❖ Don't let yourself be seen as someone who gives stress.

We learnt in earlier chapters how organisation have flavours of ego. When you are in an organisation which promotes fighting and foul language, you tend to take it as a sign of openness. Understand that fighting and shouting is not the same as having an open environment. An open environment means that you can express yourself without fear, but this expression should not be insulting to others. If you are a cause of tension for others, you are the first victim of this anger.

Join an 'Art of Living course' and get yourself out of this sickness.

❖ Follow basic etiquette.

Acknowledging mails, accepting or rejecting meeting invites, sending an invite for meeting, saying thank you when someone does some work for you, are the basic etiquettes. If you do not follow them with your team, it will very soon become your weakness. Before you realize it, you will be hated for lacking basic decencies. Initially they might seem time consuming, but actually they are not. Once you start practicing these consciously, they will boost your personality.

❖ **Understand that good ideas can indeed come from someone who does not take a fat pay cheque from you.**

This is something that is so embedded in the culture of smaller companies. They respect people based on their pay cheques. If God comes to them dressed as a common man, they will refuse to take gold from him. For these companies, a person has to be successful (and definition of success is last good drawn salary or a big brand experience) in order to accept his suggestion. This is driven out of sense of inferiority complex. While they preach, all that what matters is your good work and potential, somewhere deep inside they value brands and money alone.

No wonder most talented people who join most admired companies in their early career, continue to grow with them. This is because such a culture helps them actualize their potential. This culture values potential and talent alone.

Make an honest attempt to understand that a great idea, plan or accomplishment has nothing to do with the salary paid to the person from whom it came.

❖ Not everything calls for action.

When are you are in a leadership position, you are fed with lot of data each day.

Well, there are some inputs that are only meant to be heard, recorded, and then put on a back burner. This is because you need much more data to make any inference. You might come back to these at a later point of time.

There are some other inputs that should go straight to a dustbin.

I would strongly suggest that you do not get tempted to take action on every input. It might harm your organisation more than helping it. Also, know that there are people who form opinions based on their version of truth. Take such inputs with a pinch of salt. These are the people who will see someone sneezing and claim that he has covid. You better do a lab test first to confirm.

Chapter 10
Your Career Document

शक्तेः युक्तिः गरीयसी

"Strategy is better than strength"

If you are serious about your career growth, this tool will benefit you immensely. For that, you will need to remember all that you have read in this book so far. Keep visiting the sections and ensure you have your base covered.

While creating a career document, you start with listing strengths and improvement needs. For this, introspection, retrospection, direct feedback and 360-degree survey is to be used. Include your current organisation members, past organisation folks, and personal relationships/ friends for the same. Remember strengths and weaknesses stay with you whether you are in office or at home. At the end of the day, you are one person.

As a second step, list down long-term, mid-term, and short-term goals in that order. See that your short-term goals are useful to attain mid-term goals. And that mid-term goals are useful in your journey to attain long-term goals. Start with long-term, and then come down to short-term. On the way, you can add a few which are not related, but try to stick to the path which is ultimately leading to the accomplishment of long-term goals.

Post that, see what skills and strengths need to be targeted to attain short-term to mid-term goals. Leave the long-term goals aside for some time. Also, do not worry whether you have these strengths or not. Just write down what you think is needed for the job. If you do not know that, talk to someone who is doing that job, or observe closely those who are in that job.

Now observe what skills, strengths and limitations you have. Map them to the skills and strengths needed for you to attain short-term and mid-term goals.

Once you know what strengths and limitations you need to work on, what are the ones needed for you to get to your goals, come up with the action plan.

See what learnings, experience, etc. you need to attain a skill or gain a strength or improve upon current limitation.

Write down the actions, ETA, support needed, and measures of success.

There are two lines of thoughts on how individuals can progress.

One says work really hard on your weakness.

The other says keep building on your strength.

Actually, it depends which field you are in. If you are weak in your core skill, you should either improve in that or change your profession itself.

But in general, my advice is to polish your weakness in minimal possible time. And then whatever is absolutely needed for your growth, choose that weak skill and spend a minimum time on that.

But it is really your strength which will take you to places. Ensure you keep growing it and always bring it to the forefront, rather than keep worrying about your weakness. So, have an 80-20 rule. 80% time to grow strength further and 20% time to improve weaknesses.

Here, you have to take a pause and evaluate if within your current organisation you have the possibility to realize your goals. And whether your organisation is interested to support this journey.

It is very important to get an agreement with your manager or representative of your organisation on the support you will need to grow here.

I am attaching a template that you can use to create this plan. I would strongly recommend everyone to create one for yourself, whether you are actively working or part time employed, young or old. This this will help you in driving your life towards a destination, that will give you a sense of accomplishment. You can keep this as an evolving document and see whether you are on right path or need a course correction. Otherwise, life will be over in no time.

	Strengths	**Targeted Strengths**	**Improvement Needs**	**Targeted Improvements**
1				
2				
3				
4				
5				

	Long Term Plan			
1	Goal 1			
2	Goal 2			
	Medium Term Plan			
1	Goal 1			
2	Goal 2			
	Short Term Plan			

1	Goal 1		
2	Goal 2		
3	Goal 3		
	Actionable Items	Measure	Due Date	Support from Organisation/ Manager
1				
2				
3				

Let us understand how to fill this using an example.

Assume you are in a critical position and leading a small team. And you aim to pick up a bigger position with an additional team.

For this position, management and you have agreed that

1. Eco system needs to have confidence that you have set the current team in a way that minimum intervention is needed from your end going forward.

2. This is an area where you do not have prior experience. You want the new team to accept you as a leader, else there could be an attrition possibility.

3. In the new world, you will need to present to the client stakeholders. Your current presentation skills are not proven.

For 1, your plan should be to get right talent or grow someone from your existing team to take your current role. You have to give confidence by letting this chosen person lead in your absence. This will require active mentoring from your side.

For 2, you will need to gain techno functional expertise so that people value you for the same. Respect cannot be demanded by virtue of authority. It has to be earned. For this, you have to conduct knowledge sharing sessions for the team. This will bring credibility to your authority.

For 3, you have to improve your presentation skills and further up your communication abilities. This is hard earned. Go back to basics, start presenting to smaller known group and one fine day, you will be ready to present to the client.

Now, put a timeline to your plan and get commitment from management for the support you need to accomplish this plan.

I hope this example gives you a fair understanding of how to go about creating such plans.

You need to put your objectives for short-term, mid-term and long-term. While the detailed action plan can be short term only, planning activity should always start with long term goals, then mid-term, and finally short term.

Plans are effective only, when they have clear timelines and measurable goals. You need not restrict yourself to your current organisation while creating such a plan. But agreement and support from management becomes critical if you are looking for growth in your current organisation.

With this, you are all set to take your career to next level!

Wish you all the best!!

What Next To Expect From The Author

संगच्छध्वं

"Let us progress together"

I plan to write following books in next few years.

They cover very different subjects.

None of them will be a work of fiction.

1. "When My Father Died"

It is about my father Late Shri Sat Vrat Kaushal. He has been my ideal, someone who remained honest to the core even in an environment that was filled with filth. He was respected and loved by one and all. A Shiv bhakt, someone who prayed for well- being of anyone, whom he saw in pain. He could not think ill for anyone. His prayers worked for us, and for many others who looked upon him for help. He was an architect, sculptor, poet, painter and what not. Always an artist at heart, who lived by his name "Sat" meaning truth. He was a yogi and my first lessons in Yog asanas came from him when I was 5 years old.

He was detected with last stage cancer in 2009. He finally passed away in 2010 after more than one year of fight. He was indeed declared cancer free a few months before his death. That tells how his mental strength and fundamentals helped him beat the demon, eventually to be taken away.

The story goes around the events that unfolded, cancer as a disease, what it does to the person and his family, and the limitations of medical practice in India. This will also help those who have a cancer case around them as I will tell what is best way to go about it, what worked, and what did not work.

2. "Flying officer - Amit Kathuria"

Amit was my best friend, a childhood buddy, brother, someone who was always looked at with awe by one and all. In each other's company we lived life like a dream. We were each other's strength and it seems the universe always celebrated our companionship. When we went for a fun ride, harsh sun would turn cold, problems would look like adventure and fun. We practiced Karate together, studied alongside, played badminton, meditated, took all life decisions in unison. He was a celebrated Air force officer who just went as quickly as he had appeared in my life. In a tragedy that was so big, he along with his wife and infant son vanished in a road accident. He was one of the most amazing personalities, I have come across in my life. His fables continue to haunt till date. The story revolves around my time spent with him through our childhood, youth and then in the final moment of truth.

3. "On corporate politics"

This will bring out my entire corporate experience, my understanding of each political situation I encountered, the corporate ways, and then how things happen in this world. The focus is on the politics lying underneath. I will state a set of stories, and then dissect to understand why it happened the way it happened. And what we can learn from it.

As I was learning this subject of corporate politics, I had started predicting, and in some cases cautioning people who were in the thick of things. These experiments have helped me in validating the theories that I have developed around ways of corporate working. A small sense of what is going to be revealed is mentioned in this book around organisation culture. It should be a good read to prepare you to identify, predict, and then save yourself from corporate politics.

4. "Anatomy of a trading platform"

This will be a techno functional write up infused with culture angle to explain various architectural options available to an enterprise architect who is planning to create from scratch, or update, a trading platform. We will start with the business need. Then, we will get into the essential functional components. This will be followed by various technology choices available, and its suitability depending on the type of organisation. And then description of software applications essential to support those functional components. We will also cover the various nuts and bolts needed to bring all of this together.

We will talk about common problems faced, including anti patterns that are seen in such systems. And then talk about the common tools and patterns that can be deployed for the solution.

This will bring out over two decades of hands-on experience in working with some of the finest brains of global investment banking software industry.

5. "My own experiments with truth"

This will be my autobiography that will include topics like spirituality, health, personal life, subject of magic, politics, ethics, proof of karma theory, and a summary of corporate politics. From the time I was born to the time when I will write this book, it will have in detail what all happened, why it happened, what worked, what did not work, what to expect and what not to expect under certain conditions.

Stay Tuned!

www.ingramcontent.com/pod-product-compliance
Lightning Source LLC
LaVergne TN
LVHW061552070526
838199LV00077B/7009